Relationships

Freedom without Distance, Connection without Control

Liv Larsson

friare
LIV

www.friareliv.se

If you have not purchased this book directly from us, e-mail or call us if you wish to receive our book catalogue and newsletter.

Friare Liv AB
Mjösjölidvägen 477
946 40 Svensbyn
Sweden
Phone: + 46 911 24 11 44
info@friareliv.se
www.friareliv.se/eng

Author: Liv Larsson
Translation: Liv Larsson, Belinda Poropudas
Proofreadning; Patrica Foster
Layout: Kay Rung
Cover design: Vilhelm PH Nilsson www.communicationforlife.org/vilhelm/

ISBN printed 978-91-979442-0-5

Content

Foreword

They (the human family) will die without ever having really lived or loved. To me this is the most frightening of all possibilities. I would really hate to think that you or I might die without having really lived and really loved[1].
James Powell

Relationships have always fascinated human beings and books on relationships flood the market. Perhaps we, as James Powell said, are afraid to die without really having been touched by love, and this is the reason there are so many songs and poems written about it and so many movies made about it. We so long for this deep love, that we are willing to go through fire and water to protect it, whether it is the love of a child, a lover, a parent, or a friend. Perhaps we hope that it will heat our frozen hearts and change our lives.

I love relationships. It fascinates me to look at what connects people and what makes it possible for love to grow. However, I'm also doubtful that our learned approach to relationships can ever give us what we dream of.

This book contains a number of tools that I have used during courses about relationships over the past ten years. Even if a book has limitations in contributing to loving relationships, it may, combined with passionate devotion, work wonders. Since so many books have already been written about relationships, I have tried to simplify what I want to say in hopes of shedding some new light on what can help us to enjoy each other more.

You can use this book and its tests and exercises in any relationship. However, it is most useful in helping people evaluate and strengthen their "romantic" relationships. You can do it on your own or together with the other person involved in the relationship. The book you hold in your hands can make a difference in the relationships you care most about, so go ahead and give it a try.

Good luck!

---

1. Powell, James (1974), The Secret of Staying in Love.

Evaluating you relationships

> *What relationships are important to you?*
>
> *What are you doing today to care for them?*
>
> *Have you told those concerned how you feel?*

Most of us regularly inspect "the health" of our car. If we forget to, we miss a chance to protect not only our car but also people from accidents. In order to create the relationships you desire it is useful to at least once a year, carry out a "check – up" on your most important relationships. Take the time to do any "repair work" or "adjustments" that may prevent "accidents".

Part 1 of the "relationship evaluation" will help you to reflect on how you perceive your relationship with another person. The aim is to help you get an overview of it, and how you address different needs in your relationship.

You will get the most out of the evaluation if you and the person you choose to reflect on your relationship with, are doing it simultaneously. It will make it easier for both of you to talk about what you discover and perhaps to make some changes. It is beneficial if the other person is willing to reflect up on your relationship, but if not, you will still get a lot out of doing it on your own. You can gain valuable details about what you would do differently or what you want to ask of the other person. Remember that a relationship is not static, meaning that each evaluation is a "snapshot photo" which captures only what is happening in the moment, even if there may be things that keep reoccurring in the relationship.

There are no wrong or right answers; it is not about judging the relationship as good or bad, but about evaluating how well your needs are met.

The moment you start reflecting on your relationship, change is already happening and the situation has already changed. If you do another evaluation in two weeks time you will discover something very different from the last evaluation.

To really make the reflection meaningful, you need a little time to focus, so please be sure to find a place that allows you to sit in peace and quiet.

Start with Part 1 and then decide if you want to proceed with any of the other parts. Be attentive as to whether there are any specific questions that touched you or made you reflect deeper. It is important that you do not share some parts of the answers with the other person, without first having done some work on them yourself.

Instructions: Choose a *specific* relationship when you answer the questions. If you have more than one relationship you want to reflect on, focus on each one at a time. If you find yourself wanting to skip questions that do not seem relevant or meaningful, or even have difficulty answering, or do not find any response to at all, you may find that they have something important to tell you. Since what is requested in Part 1 of the "relationship evaluation" is to identify if needs are met or not?

I would like to take a few words to describe what I mean by "needs". What I mean by the word "need" is something that all humans share. Needs are something innate, and universal, and which motivate us to act in life-serving ways. We could say that needs are the "essence of life". All human behavior stems from attempts to meet our needs and these needs are never in conflict. If people can identify their needs, the needs of others, and the feelings that surround these needs, it will be easier to connect and build relationships in satisfying ways.

Needs are not tied to a person, place, time nor to a specific act but can be seen and met in a variety of ways. For example, I may get my need for love met when I get a hug from someone, or through singing, dancing, having sex, or by playing with children out in nature. The need for community can be met with different people. And the need for autonomy or freedom, in the way I use it here, can be experienced both if you are alone and if you are together with others, and even if you are imprisoned.

It is with this view of the word "need" that I suggest you do the relationship evaluation. Read more under "Assumptions that help us to create satisfying relationships" and review a list of common needs on page 27.

Relationship evaluation - Part 1 Basic evaluation

1. On a scale of 1-6, identify how important it is to you that the following needs are met in an intimate relationship.

	Not so important					Very important
Love	1	2	3	4	5	6
Meaning	1	2	3	4	5	6
Intimacy	1	2	3	4	5	6
Respect	1	2	3	4	5	6
Safety	1	2	3	4	5	6
Freedom	1	2	3	4	5	6
Honesty	1	2	3	4	5	6
Understanding	1	2	3	4	5	6
Passion	1	2	3	4	5	6
To have fun	1	2	3	4	5	6
Unity	1	2	3	4	5	6
Inspiration	1	2	3	4	5	6
Community	1	2	3	4	5	6
To be seen and heard	1	2	3	4	5	6
Other need(s) _____	1	2	3	4	5	6

2.   On a scale from 1-6, identify how well these needs are usually met in the relationship you have chosen to evaluate.

	Seldom met				Often met	
Love	1	2	3	4	5	6
Meaning	1	2	3	4	5	6
Intimacy	1	2	3	4	5	6
Respect	1	2	3	4	5	6
Safety	1	2	3	4	5	6
Freedom	1	2	3	4	5	6
Honesty	1	2	3	4	5	6
Understanding	1	2	3	4	5	6
Passion	1	2	3	4	5	6
To have fun	1	2	3	4	5	6
Unity	1	2	3	4	5	6
Inspiration	1	2	3	4	5	6
Community	1	2	3	4	5	6
To be seen and heard	1	2	3	4	5	6
Other need(s) _____	1	2	3	4	5	6

3. Compare how you circled numbers in the first two tables and highlight any differences.

4a. Which of your needs are most satisfied in this relationship?

b. Have you told the other person about these needs?

If you have not, ask yourself if you want to do it now and in what way?

5a. What are the needs that are especially important for you to have met in this relationship and what contributes to meeting them?

b. If these needs are not being met in the relationship, are there any requests you want to express to that person? To yourself? To someone else?

6a. Which of your needs are the least satisfied in the relationship?

b. Is it important for you to find ways to have these needs met more often in this relationship?

If yes, c. Are there any requests you want to express to the other person, which might help them to provide concrete steps to meet those needs (b)?

d. Are there any requests you want to express to someone else who could help you to meet these needs (b)?

7a. What helps you to experience love and meaning in this relationship?

b. Is there anything you can ask this person about that you think would help you to better meet your needs for love and meaning?

If you are making this evaluation with another person, you can share your responses and insights. Focus on the parts that seem most important to you.

Continue with part 2 or any other part you are interested in. If parts 2-6 do not feel meaningful at the moment, I suggest that you at least use the time for part 7 and look at what you actually do to meet your needs.

If you have been doing the evaluation on your own, you can continue with Part 2 or any other part that interests you.

The Potential of Relationships

Imagine that you are extremely well prepared for an important mission in Paris. You have your mind set on the goal, you have rented a Vespa, you have learned some key phrases in French, you're in good time and you have a city map in your hand. But whatever you do, you cannot find your destination. You're getting more and more stressed and you are running faster and faster. The frustration is increasing at the thought of all the preparation you have done and yet now nothing seems to work. You have learned that you should think positively, so you smile, try to shake off the frustration and keep looking. Finally, after a few hours of this frustrating process, you discover that the map you have in your hand is not a map of Paris, but one of Brussels.

Perhaps the most important insight we can have when it comes to relationships is to recognize that the map we navigate by may not always be true to the terrain. If you are trying to use a map that is not showing you where you are, you can put an enormous amount of time and energy into getting your relationships to work without ever feeling satisfied. All tools, whatever they are, become superfluous, unless you have a map that is consistent with reality. You can get deeply involved, have a positive attitude and put lots of time into "managing" your relationships, but if you have a distorted view of the possibilities and limits of what a relationship can give you, it means that you will never experience the relationship as satisfactory.

If you think you are automatically going to be eternally happy if you fall in love with a person who falls in love with you, you are probably going to be disappointed. After a while, it is possible that you discover that your happiness in the relationship was not solid, which you may translate into the idea that you have not found the "right person" - and so you leave to look for the right one. Relationships are more complicated than that and we need to make deposits if we want to make withdrawals. So before you move on - take a moment to consider these questions:

What do you dream about in your closest relationships?

What do you hope to get out of them?

Are you prepared to work with the relationship?

Is this realistic? Likely? Then go for it!

And they lived happily ever after ...?

Many of us seem to think that love relationships automatically make us happier. If we only find the "right one", we will live in a permanent euphoria. Most stories and movies end in the pink glow of the relationships beginning, with the promise of living happily ever after ringing in our ears. The Prince gets the Princess and half of the kingdom, and then the story ends, as if everything will now remain just as it was at that moment.

"Yes, yes, but if I meet the right one it will be different. The right one will make me happy. When I meet him or her, everything will be so much easier. Those who talk about this having to "work on a relationship", just have not yet met the true love of their life.

A study done in Germany with 25, 000 people over 15 years of age, showed that marriage and long-term relationships only had a temporary effect on human happiness. For about two years after a wedding the happiness level was higher than before, but then it went back to the same level as the people had before they married.[2] It would be nice if all those love songs and films were true, if it was just as simple

---

2. The How of Happiness - A Scientific Approach to Getting the Life You Want By Sonja Lyubomirsky Penguin Putnam Inc.

as finding the "right one". The idea of finding the "best" or the "right one" is based on the same mind set applied in many areas of our culture. We should have "the best ', "the latest fashion", "the latest update." It is not surprising if we continue to think in similar ways about relationships. Relations between us become uncertain when we start worrying about being replaced with a more "updated" version. We may even begin to look for a "new version" ourselves, be it a new friend or a new partner. Thinking that there is something such as "the right person" can lead us to consume relationships with friends and lovers as we consume computers. After two years when they are not new anymore, we will replace them with a new one.

> *Almitra spake again and said,*
> *And what of Marriage, master?*
> *And he answered saying:*
> *You were born together, and together you shall be forevermore.*
> *You shall be together when the white wings of death scatter your days.*
> *Ay, you shall be together even in the silent memory of God.*
> *But let there be space in your togetherness,*
> *And let the winds of the heavens dance*
> *between you.*
> *Even as the strings of a lute are alone though they quiver with the same music.*
>
> *Love one another, but make not a bond of love:*
> *Let it rather be a moving sea between the shores of your souls.*
> *Fill each other's cup but drink not from one cup.*
> *Give one another of your bread but eat not from the same loaf.*
> *Sing and dance together and be joyous, but let each one of you be alone,*
> *Give your hearts, but not into each other's keeping..*
> *For only the hand of Life can contain your hearts.*
> *And stand together yet not too near together:*
> *For the pillars of the temple stand apart,*
> *And the oak tree and the cypress grow not in each other's shadow.*
>
> Gibran Kahlil, "The Prophet"

To be seen as Mr or Mrs "Right" is not always easy. It may produce a lot of pressure, because disappointment is not far away when the expectation is that everything will be as perfect as in a romantic movie. We are no longer making conscious choices about how we communicate if our thoughts are based on ideas such as: *"If you love me you will understand me and can hear my good intentions, even if I criticize you."*

We might say yes to going on holiday together on the sole ground that "if only we are together then everything will be okay." And if the holiday turns into a failure, we begin to ask ourselves if this person really is "the right one". We have, as Gibran warned in the text above, been allowing the temple pillars to lean towards each other with the effect that the ceiling starts caving in.

A relationship based on the idea that if we have found "the right one" can be like living with a ticking bomb. There are many relationships that cannot take that pressure. When the romantic image that we have in the beginning of a relationship is replaced by everyday life, it is easy to give up. If we stay in the relationship, it is easy to be critical of everything the other does, and if we leave, we then continue to search for "the Right one".

A study from Heriot-Watt University in Edinburgh shows that many are disappointed with their relationship after comparing themselves with romantic movies that involve fate, love at first sight and finding the dream prince or princess. Relationships need work to keep them healthy and vibrant and true love requires more than fireworks, red roses and chocolate. Our unrealistic expectations can often make it difficult for us to see what we can do to maintain love and closeness.

I am not suggesting that we refrain from romantic relationships, or from things we call "romantic" but that it can be useful to take a look at what is actually needed to nurture love and warmth in relationships. One way is to regularly ask the question, *"What can I do to enrich your life?"*

Relationship evaluation - Part 2 How can we enrich each other's lives?

Do part 2 first alone, and then share some of the responses with the other person if you want to.

Step 1 - "What can I do to enrich your life?"

Focus on your connection with a person close to you. Imagine that you're talking to that person and that she or he is interested in what you have to say.

8a. Imagine asking the other: "What can I do that would make a difference for you? How can I enrich your life?"

Write down what you imagine the other would answer.

b. Then ask (still in the imagined situation): "Have you told me this before? "

If the person answers "yes", ask: In what way did you express it to me at that time?

If the person answers "no", ask: "What is it that has been in the way of you telling me this before?

Write down the answer.

Step 2 - "What can you do to enrich my life?"

9 a. Imagine that you are getting the same questions from the other person: "What can I do that would make a difference for you? How can I enrich your life?"

Write down your answer:

b. The person asks (still in the imagined situation): "Have you told me this before?"

If you answer yes, then answer also how you expressed it at that time.

If you answer is "no" then also tell what prevented you from telling this to her or him before.

Step 3

If you do this exercise with the other person, share with each other what you have discovered and how you answered the different questions. Even if the other person has not done it, you can talk about it with him or her, but remember that it might take him or her some time to reflect on it. First ask if she or he wants to hear your thoughts on how you can help each other in ways you might not have thought of so far. Or ask the question: "What can I do to enrich your life?"

If the person has not done this exercise, this may seem new and strange. Take it slowly and pause when one or both of you need time to integrate what you've talked about. You may also want to spend some time on your own for step 4.

Step 4 – Reflection

Take some time for yourself to reflect on what you've learned, about yourself, about how you want to contribute, about relationships and about the other person. Is there some request you want to make of yourself?

Happy Together

The most beautiful thing I can imagine is to contribute to people who are close to me in becoming as happy as possible. So if my partner's main "happiness strategy" is to enjoy life through food, music and forest walks, I can support him or her in doing this. If my friend becomes restless and unhappy if she or he does not take the time for daily exercise, I can help him or her to find time for this.

I can also ask for support in what makes me happy. In this way my partner or friend gets a chance to also have the fun of contributing to me.

A happy relationship implies happy individuals. Sonja Lyubomirsky has compiled research on 12 different happiness strategies which she describes in detail in her book The How of Happiness.[3]

Research has shown that one of the strategies that make us happy is "Nurturing relationships". So the relationship itself does not necessarily make you happy, but focusing on nurturing it can. Happiness research has shown that this strategy increases the happiness level for some people more than for others. As you have chosen to read this book, you probably have an interest in nurturing relationships, maybe because you've noticed that it makes you happier. You cannot, however, expect the same interest from those close to you. Often we interpret disinterest in "working with the relationship" as proof that the relationship is not important to that person. But perhaps it is simply that he or she does not experience increased happiness by focusing on nurturing relationships. In the box on the next page the 12 happiness strategies that Lyubomirsky has compiled in her research are listed.

---

3. The How of Happiness - A Scientific Approach to Getting the Life You Want By Sonja Lyubomirsky Penguin Putnam Inc

Happiness strategies

- Expressing gratitude.

- Cultivating optimism.

- Avoiding overthinking and social comparison.

- Performing acts of kindness.

- Nurturing relationships.

- Develop strategies for coping.

- Learning to forgive and to listen with empathy.

- Doing activites that truly engage you (Flow).

- Savoring life´s joys.

- Committing to your goals.

- Practicing religion and spirituality.

- Taking care of your body through meditation.

What can you do to help the people closest in your life to do more of what makes them happy?

Is there any support you could ask for concerning what makes you happy?

Assumptions that help us to create satisfying relationships

The following assumptions about people and communication can be used as support when you want to connect with others in a compassionate way. If you want to nurture your relationship, I suggest that you choose actions based on these assumptions. They are not to be held as truths, but as opportunities and inspiration to communicate and relate in new ways. The inspiration for them is found in Nonviolent Communication (NVC).[4]

Human beings share the same needs

When I relate to other people as if they have the same basic needs as I do, it becomes easier to feel compassion for and understanding of our differences. It makes it easier to see that conflict is not about the needs in themselves, but that conflict arises from the different strategies we choose to meet our needs.

Everyone's needs are important

Awareness that we cannot fully meet our needs, if it is at the expense of others, makes it easier for us to act in a more supporting and compassionate way. If we consider everyone's needs, including our own, as important, our relationships will be characterized by mutual interest and respect. Everyone will benefit when everyone's needs are considered important.

Emotions tell us what we need

All feelings give us clues about what we need. When needs are met, we feel joy, satisfaction, peace or excitement. When they are not met, we feel sadness, fear or anxiety. If we relate what we feel to what we need (instead of linking it to what we think others have done wrong) we are no longer going to blame others. Instead of using our energy

---

4 www.cnvc.org, www.friareliv.se.

in trying to get others to change, we use it to try to meet our needs. Distinguishing between what we think about a situation from what we feel, makes it easier for others to understand what we need and to have compassion for others and ourselves.

Human action is motivated by a desire to meet needs

Resorting to violence is an attempt (even if it's a tragic one), to meet needs. If we can meet our needs in ways that do not harm others, we prefer to choose that way. Even if our needs are not met, the connection with needs can sometimes be enough to be okay with a situation. We try to meet needs without demanding that anyone do anything they do not want to do, as this would not meet their needs.

People enjoy contributing

It is in our nature to enjoy contributing to others, if we feel free to also say no. Coercion does not lead to more needs being met. One way of experiencing more freedom in our intimate relationships is to transform demands, both our own and others, into requests.

When we listen for what others feel to get some ideas about what they need, we will no longer hear criticism or feel guilt or shame. This makes it easier for us to understand how we can contribute. At the same time it will make it easier to say no, because it is clear that we are not responsible for other people's needs being met.

To distinguish observations from interpretations gives us a common reality

If we see the difference between the actions of others and our interpretations of them, it becomes easier to manage conflict and to appreciate differences. We have learnt to make judgments based on right and wrong when our needs are not met. Instead of believing the content of these judgments, we can use them as signals of needs not being met.

If we see people as free to choose, it will make it easier to relate to their choices

If we refrain from trying to control others and from using words that suggest that anyone "must," "should," or "can not" do something, we have a better chance to build relationships based on freedom, genuine care, compassion and respect. We then see people as responsible for their choices and that they are free to choose how to act. It is often easier for them to make new choices if they get more information or are approached with empathy. Whatever the circumstances, we can meet our need for autonomy in choosing how we want to relate to the situation we are in. We can continue to express preferences rather than demands, even when others say no to something we have asked for. We focus on finding solutions that will meet everyone's needs, not just our own, and not just those of others.

Conflicts are handled more easily if we prioritize connection

If we prioritize connection instead of trying to find solutions to a conflict, it provides space for security, learning and respect. People want to feel more important than "results", and are often willing to let go of their positions if they feel that they as persons are important.

All people have the ability to experience and show compassion

We all have an innate ability to feel compassion. But we do not always have the skills needed to convey this compassion. Compassion is "contagious", so when we are treated with compassion and respect it usually brings out our ability to relate to others in the same way. The more compassion the greater the ability to meet needs in peaceful ways.

Characteristics of relationships whose purpose is to enrich life

1. We are aware that we are mutually dependent and value others' needs being met as much as our own. We know that our needs can not be cared for at someone else's expense, without affecting the relationship negatively.

2. We show empathy for what others feel and need, and for what we feel and need, instead of blaming ourselves and others.

3. We take care of ourselves and each other with a single purpose: to enrich life. We try to not motivate ourselves or others by force of any kind, guilt, shame, duty, demands, threat of punishment or promise of external rewards.

I do not recognize you!

Something that can make a relationship stagnate and become lifeless are the labels we use on each other and the diagnoses and analyzes we make about each other.

We can approach all static thinking with the idea that it carries information about how we can bring more life into the relationship. To find the information, we need to devote time to "translating" or "decoding" labels and analysis. What do we really want to say when we call someone lazy, fantastic, greedy, or a freedom addict? The answer can be found in the observations, feelings, needs and requests that are behind these labels.

Our judgments of others can show us what we need, dream about and long for, if we listen for it instead of believing our judgment to be true or not.

If we judge ourselves because we are judging someone else, we start a carousel of judgments. I am therefore not suggesting that we stop judging, but that we use our judgments to understand what we need.

All static ideas of anyone, whether they are "positive" or "negative" set expectations. If I see you as "lazy", I expect you to say no if I ask you for help. If I see you as "helpful" and you say no, I may think about you this way: "Now I do not recognize you, you always use to help out!".

I have great respect for the pain it may stimulate in others if we express our judgements about them. It can be a pretty daunting task to rebuild trust and care in relationships when judgements are expressed, especially if they come from a person who is important to you. I suggest that you refrain from expressing labels, judgments or interpretation you have about the other, directly to them. Express only the observations, feelings, needs and requests behind the judgements. If someone persists in wanting to hear your judgments, it may be because they yearn to hear more about how they affect you. Try to express this without talking about some static images of them.

One way that you can notice if you have mixed observations with interpretations, is if you are using the verb "to be" when you talk about the other. Whenever you say that "she or he is like this or like that" you know you have mixed an interpretation into your observation. This is also true when you say "you should be more..." or "she should be less ...".

Do Part 2 of the relationship evaluation with a person other than the one you are evaluating your relationship with. Help each other and use the lists of feelings and needs on the next page to get clarity about what you feel and need.

Every label can give us a clue about what we are feelings and needing. If I for example, I put the label "selfish" on someone, it can be that I feel sad because I have a need of care or warmth. Behind the label "lazy" I might be feeling disappointed and the need may be for support or cooperation. Note that there are no "right answers" or that there is always a certain feeling or a specific need behind a particular label. You need to take the time to look behind every label and find the feeling behind it, and to let it show you what you need.

Feelings mixed with thoughts are a description of emotions mixed with our labels and analysis about others and their intentions. If you use words as the ones from the list below, it might be challenging to connect, both with yourself and others:

Attacked, rejected, betrayed, neglected, dominated, insulted, manipulated, misunderstood, neglected, unwanted, let down, inferior, run over, superior, abandoned.

Usual emotions when our need are met

Amazed	Fulfilled	Joyous	Stimulated
Comfortable	Glad	Moved	Surprised
Confident	Hopeful	Optimistic	Thankful
Eager	Inspired	Proud	Touched
Energetic	Intrigued	Relieved	Trustful

Usual emotions when our need are not met

Angry	Discouraged	Hopeless	Overwhelmed
Annoyed	Distressed	Impatient	Puzzled
Concerned	Embarrassed	Irritated	Reluctant
Confused	Frustrated	Lonely	Sad
Disappointed	Helpless	Nervous	Uncomfortable

Some exampels of human needs

Autonomy
- Choosing dreams/goals/values
- Choosing plans for fulfilling one's dreams, goals, values

Celebration
- Celebrating the creation of life and dreams fulfilled
- Celebrating losses: loved ones, dreams, etc. (mourning)

Integrity
- Authenticity • Creativity
- Meaning • Self-worth

Interdependence
- Acceptance
- Appreciation
- Closeness
- Community
- Consideration
- Contribution to the enrichment of life
- Emotional Safety
- Empathy
- Respect
- Trust

Physical Nurturance
- Air
- Food
- Movement, exercise
- Protection from life-threatening forms of life: viruses, bacteria, insects, predatory animals
- Rest
- Sexual expression
- Shelter
- Touch
- Water

Play
- Fun • Laughter

Spiritual Communion
- Beauty
- Harmony
- Inspiration
- Peace
- Honesty (the empowering honesty that enables us to learn from our limitations)
- Love
- Support
- Understanding

Relationship evaluation - Part 3
Beyond the static images

Do **not** do the first part of Part 3 together with the person you are exploring your labels on. When you come to the needs and requests, you can express them. DO NOT EXPRESS any labels and analysis because they often damage the relationship more than they benefit it! It can be tempting to ask to hear them or to express them, but if you really care about the relationship, don't do it!

Use clear measurable observations of what you saw the other person do or heard them say, and add them to your feelings, needs and requests. By observation, I mean for example, quoting something you heard the other person say, or something you've seen him or her do, where you do not mix in interpretations. Don't express any ideas of what the other person's intentions were, as this usually leads to disconnection.

Step 1

10a. Which labels and judgments do you have about the other person? In what way do you think they affect the other person and your relationship?

b.   What labels do you think the other person has put on you? In what way do they affect your relationship with him or her?

c.   Which observations? feelings? needs? and requests are behind the labels you put on the other person? (Please use the feelings and needs lists for support on page 26 - 27)

d.   What observations, feelings, needs and requests do you think are behind the labels that the other person puts on you?
Steps c and d are done for each label you want to translate and transform. Start with labels that have some charge, positively or

negatively. Get help from someone else (other then the person involved) to find the feelings and needs.

Step 2

Before expressing any of the things you have found, with the person concerned, ask yourself these questions: *Is my intention in expressing these to enrich and strengthen the relationship?"*

If the answer is "no", do not share with this person right away. Make sure to share what is going on inside you with a friend or someone who can listen to you with empathy, in order to check that what you want to share will be beneficial for the relationship.

If the answer is "yes" and it is clear that you want to communicate in an attempt to deepen the connection and strengthen the relationship ask the other: *"I want a deeper connection with you and would like to share some things I long for in our relationship, would you be interested in hearing what I have to say?"*

Take it gently, listen with empathy for any reaction that comes up for the other person when you share.

And remember: Do not express the labels but only the observations you made and the requests, feelings and needs that you trust can create connection!

Freedom

If we hear what someone says as a demand or as an expectation, we can take it as a signal that we have lost touch with what the other person is feeling and needing. We cannot hear need and demands at the same time, because they belong to two different paradigms.

It is useful to realize that when you hear a demand in something that someone expresses, you know that you can redirect your attention on trying to understand what the other person is longing for, behind what you perceive to be a demand.

Of course it is easier to hear demands if someone says "You have no choice, you have to..." or "You must ..." than if they tell you what they need and what they would like to ask from you. But you always have a choice to listen for what someone needs, no matter how they express themselves.

Love does not grow under coercion. As soon as I think, say or act in order to get someone to do something, even though they do not want it, it risks threatening their sense of love, and also their need for freedom, care and respect.

Love is stimulated by freedom. I have often heard people who have just fallen in love say: "I love the freedom I feel with this person," or "I've never felt so free before."

And after two or three years I have heard the same people express how frustrated they are at the other person's desire for freedom or how they are trying to control and limit each other. It is natural to have expectations that we should be treated with care and respect. We are born with expectations - that other people will help us to meet our needs. When we grow up we learn a language that often makes us confuse these expectations with the idea that our needs can only be met if a particular person does something, and that this needs to happen right now. Expectations and trust, change into demands. If our need for freedom is not met, the relationship becomes progressively more and more lifeless. Expectations are more indirect than demands and often do not raise as strong a reaction as demands do. But it will nonetheless, slowly suck the marrow out of the relationship when we take things for granted or begin to make demands.

When we experience demand, we have two choices; either we rebel or we submit. We either say no and close off communication, or we agree to things we do not want. People in different settings and cultures have shown that they are prepared to die to experience freedom, that is how important it is that freedom and autonomy are recognized. It is not an aspect of human nature to want to be a slave.

Linda was not clear if she wanted to stay in a relationship with Peter. In a letter to me she wrote:

Many people see our relationship as a very free one. If one of us wants to buy something, travel somewhere or do something on our own, we tend to support each other. When someone wants to go to the cinema or to a party we might go together, but if one of us does not feel like it, it's never a problem. But oddly enough I still do not feel as free as I would like to. I long for some kind of inner freedom and space - to be myself just as I am. It feels like I'm about to lose all joy in our relationship and I cannot really see what to do.

When I later met with Linda she told me about how Peter had expectations that she should feel a certain way. As a result she often did not show what she really felt and that in turn led to a great sense of loneliness for her. Although she repeatedly heard him say that he wanted her to have a good time, it was often hard for her to completely trust it. It could be a glance he gave her, when she was irritated, or that he kept a distance when she was sad, or the tone of voice he used when he said "have fun" to her when she left for some meeting with a friend.

The times she decided to take Peter's words seriously and told him the things she would like to be different. It often ended in him hearing what she said as criticism. It could be that she pointed out he had left dirty coffee mugs in front of the TV and asked him to wash them. These situations often ended with a quarrel in which he could say something like, "You get so upset about such small things. I would like you to see what I actually do. You need to learn to relax and let me be who I am! " She usually left the situation silently thinking that is was true that he did not care about her.

When we met it was clear that both of them had refrained from asking the other things, as they did not want to be perceived as demanding. Their unexpressed requests, especially Linda's about being heard about how she wanted things, had "gone sour" and once she expressed it, it often sounded like a demand. I helped them express some requests and they were amazed at how good they both felt to actually hear a clear request from the other. This was different than living with a creeping sense of unspoken expectations.

It took them time to learn to say "no I do not want this" when they didn't want something, without worrying that it might be perceived as criticism. They also were able to know when to say yes, because they really wanted it, and not because they "should". They learned as well to recognize when they were about to say "yes" or to agree to anything because they should "prove" that they had such a free relationship.

And they gained more trust that what the other said was what they meant and nothing else. They learned how to handle a "no", without giving upon their needs. They realized that they could continue to communicate to find a third solution, which meant that they did not need to say yes to anything they did not want.

What touched me most with how they worked on this was how much more love they told me they experienced when their requests were expressed, and they could trust one another.

In addition, they both indicated that they felt they were more important to the other person in a completely different way than before.

About requests

When we ask someone for something that would help us meet our needs, it may be worthwhile to consider a few things:

1. When you ask others to change a behavior, connect by asking how she or he feels when you express yourself or make a certain request. Follow up your requests with:
   "I would like to hear what you are feeling when you hear what I say, are you willing to tell me?"

2. You can also connect by asking the other person to tell you what he or she has heard that is important to you. You do this by expressing something like:
   "Now that I've expressed this, I would like to be sure that it is clear to you what I feel and need in relation to it. Are you willing to tell me what you have understood that my feelings and needs are?"

It might feel strange to ask someone to repeat what he or she has heard you say. But, for example, for air traffic controllers, military officers and surgical staff it is a part of everyday life to repeat important information. This is especially important in "emergency situations" where life-threatening danger is possible if we do not have accurate information. These professions have embraced the knowledge that our brains add information in order to get the bigger picture to match, sometimes with disastrous effects.

In such extreme situations, it is easy to see the value of extra clarity. And at the same time isn't it our intimate relationships that make our life meaningful? Why not make use of this knowledge to protect what is most valuable to us?

3. Minimize the risk that others hear what you say as a demand. You can do this by avoiding words such as "must", "should", "have to" or "deserve", but above all by being clear that you are willing to accept a "No."

    When someone does something you ask for, not because they want to help you, but to avoid feeling shame, guilt, or because they are afraid of being punished, it harms your relationship. Others lose the joy of helping you when they hear what you are asking for as a demand. It can take a lot of energy to repair the connection if this type of communication has been going on for a long time.

4. Minimize confusion by being specific about whom, when, and how, when you make a request. Here it is useful to think of how to express what you do want, rather than what you do not want. It is also worthwhile to check if the request that you are expressing is really possible to do. For example, the request "I want you to respect me" could be difficult. "I would feel more respect if you would ask me if I'm willing to lend you my clothes, instead of just taking them. Is there anything that is in the way of you asking me this?", more clearly expresses what it is that you want.

5. Make it easier for others to understand what they are contributing to, if she or he says yes to what you ask for. When you tell others

what needs of yours would be met by the person doing what you requested, it will be easier for them to find the motivation to contribute to your needs being met.

When you express what you feel (sad), what you need (belonging) and what you want from the other person (would you like to be at home with me tonight for three hours?) It becomes clearer to him or her what a yes contributes to.

Save a bush

I was on my way to do a few days of training and as I jumped into the car I asked my partner, who was out in the garden, to do something about some bushes that were disturbing the view from the house.

"Would you cut down those bushes while you're out here"? I asked, making a sweeping gesture at knee height to show how high I wanted the two elderberry bushes.

"Yes"! he answered quickly.

The first thing I saw when I got home after two days, made me first stare and then laugh. On the ground where one of the bushes had grown there was just a hole. There was not a trace that this place had ever had a bush growing here. The second bush was still growing strong, appearing more radiant than ever. I curiously asked my partner what had happened to the missing bush.

He said proudly *"It was not easy, but now it is gone!"*

How could this have happened? Whose fault was it? Who was responsible for the missing bush?

Was it my fault because I was not clear what I had wanted, or because I did not take time to make sure that I was understood? Or was it my partner's fault because he did not make sure he really got what I wanted?

Instead of looking for whose fault misunderstandings are, it is more meaningful if we instead think about what we can learn from the mistakes made. What could I have done differently? In addition to cutting the trees myself, hiring a gardener or letting the bushes grow (advice I have often heard when I've told this story), I could have been more specific:

"I want you to cut both of them to 40 cm in height."

Or, if I was too stressed to figure that out, I could have made a call from the car and said:

"Hey, I was a bit stressed so I am unsure if it was clear what I asked of you, would you tell me what you heard?"

The bush's life could have been saved. What could my partner have done? Being also concerned that we were both happy with our home, he could have reflected on what he had heard me asking for. He could have said something like:

"Do you mean you want me to cut down the right bush, the one that is right in front of the window, completely"?

Relationship evaluation - Part 4
Expectations and demands

Do this part of the relationship evaluation regularly to clear the relationship of demands and to transform expectations that might turn up every now and then. Reflect on your own answers to the questions (step 1) and then talk about what you've discovered together (step 2).

Remember that this is not a training on how to make fewer requests - perhaps it will lead to even more of them: It is about making clear present requests and clearing them from demands. It is more likely that the other person will want to do what we ask for, if they experience it as voluntary.

Step 1:

11a. What kind of expectations about and demands of you do you think the other person has?

b. What makes you believe this?
What has the other person actually said or done that makes you think that those expectations are there? Quote something she or he has said, or describe what you have seen her or him do. Be sure to distinguish your observations from your interpretation that she or he has demanded something from you.

c. What do you feel when you think about what you have heard or seen him or her do (your answers to point b)?

d. Which of your needs do you think he or she is trying to meet by doing what he or she does or says?

e. Which of your needs are met or not met by the action (b)?

f. Is there anything you would like to express around this to the other person? Something you want to ask for that could meet both your needs and his or her needs?

12a. What are your expectations of the other person? What do you think that she or he "should" do? Or "should not" do? What do you demand that he or she has to do?

b. In what ways have you expressed this to the other person? If you have not expressed the demands or expectations directly - what have you expressed instead? Quote yourself or describe how you have acted, keeping it clear of interpretation.

c. What do you feel when you think about this?

d. Which of your needs, do you hope will be met by thinking or communicating that the person "should" act differently from what she or he does? (A)

e. Are there any needs of the other person that you hope will be met by him or her changing their behavior?

b. Is there anything you would like to express to him or her now that you've explored this?

13a. What expectations and demands do you think the other person experiences from you?

b. How would you guess that this makes him or her feel?

c. What needs do you think will be met or not met?

d. Is there anything you would like to express to him or her around this?

14a. What are your expectations and demands of yourself in relationship to him or her? Are they in any way linked to her or his expectations?

b. What do you feel when you think about it?

c. Which of your needs are met or not met by this?

d. Is there anything you would like to express or request now? Of the other person or from someone else?

Step 2

Before bringing up any of the insights that you had in step 1 with whom it may concern, ask yourself these questions: *"Is my intention to express this, anchored in my wish to enrich and strengthen the relationship?"*

If the answer is a "no" wait before you share this with the other person. Be sure though, to share what is going on inside you with a friend or someone who can listen to you with empathy.

When the answer is "yes" and it is clear that you want to communicate in an attempt to create more connection and strengthen the relationship, ask the other person: *"I would like to share some things with you that I hope will bring more connection and joy into our relationship, would you like to hear what I want to say?"*

Take it slowly, listen to any response with empathy and express feelings, needs, and any requests that come up when you express what you have discovered. Be especially careful:

1. to express requests and not demands.

2. to express yourself in way that help the other person to hear requests and not demands.

3. to clarify what needs you are hoping will bet met by your requests.

If you loved me, you would get me the bread

Are you willing to get us some more bread? my partner asked me one morning at the breakfast table and pointed at the pantry.

"No", I replied, after a moment of hesitation,*" as I just started eating my breakfast, and I am sitting so comfortably right now and would like to enjoy just sitting for a while."*

At hearing 'no', my partner noticed he got irritated. Looking closer at his thought, he realized that he was thinking: "She is sitting so much closer, why can't she even do such a small thing for me ...!??"

Then he noticed that his irritation had turned into disappointment and that he had translated my behavior thus: "This is proof that she doesn't love me, such a small thing and she finds no joy in doing it for me."

Then his disappointment turned into sadness and it was then that he realized he even had some idea that his evaluation was the truth. At that same point he also realized the absurdity of linking my un-willingness to get him bread with a lack of love. The expectation was particularly absurd because I did not even know it would be inter-preted as a sign of love from me.

At the same time something was going on inside of my head: "How nice it is to be able to say "no" when I mean "no" and "yes" when I mean "yes"! I would love to feel this free in all my relationships.

These internal dialogues could have passed us by if my partner had not wondered why I was smiling while enjoying the inner freedom I experienced.

"What are you smiling at?" he asked.

"I am smiling because I so enjoy the sense of freedom I feel when I can be totally honest with you", I said and told him how nice it was to be able to say no when I just wanted to sit instead of getting up.

Now it was his turn to smile and my turn to ask where his smile came from. He told me his discovery that me not getting the bread, not only meant that he would have to get up and get it himself but that it was a proof that I did not love him:

I also realized that you don't even know what has just gone through my head and how you just demonstrated to me how your not getting the bread has nothing to do with your love for me!

If he had told me that he longed to experience love and care and that I could help him to experience this if I got the bread I would probably have been very willing to get it. My partner realized that before this incidence he had even learned to think that if I would have gotten the bread before he even asked for it, it would have been the highest proof of my love for him. He had learnt that if someone did something even though they did not really want to, but did it "for the sake of others", it was the ultimate proof of love.

Through this experience, we had had an opportunity to talk about how we could create more chances to express or receive love. If somebody else would have asked, I would probably have gotten the bread, although I did not want to, and then silently accused the other person of being demanding or lazy. It would probably have led to less love, not more.

What are you afraid to ask for in fear of getting a "no"?

What do you experience as a challenge to saying "no" to?

No!!!

The fear of receiving a "no" can make it a challenge to express a clear request. But what exactly is it that makes it so dreadful to be met with a "no"? One of the reasons that it might be difficult to express requests is that we have learned that if someone says no to what we are asking for, it says something about us.

We have learned to interpret a 'no' as a rejection. And to be rejected means there is something wrong with us. To avoid the shame of not being worthy of a "yes", we often stop asking for what we need. We can also avoid saying "no" for the same reason. We want to support people, especially those close to us, and we are afraid that if we say no to them that they will see us as someone who doesn't see them as worthy of a "yes". But when we say yes, without really wanting to, in the long term it can be very costly, as there will be a loss of trust and willingness to do things for the other person on our part.

Three valuable assumptions

1. Every "no" is a "yes" to something else.

2. Saying "no" can be heard as an invitation to further dialogue.

3. There is always more than one way to meet needs.

Let me show you how I use these three assumptions:

1. Behind every "no" there is a "yes" to something else.

If I ask you if you want to go swimming with me and you say "no", I can hear that there is a need of yours that you do not believe will be fulfilled by saying yes. Your "no" may be a "yes" to your needs for freedom or relaxation, as you would like to spend your time finishing a project that is important to you. If I connect to this, I will be less likely to hear your no to be about me or as a rejection.

2. Saying no is an invitation to further dialogue.

If I hear your "no" as an invitation to further dialogue, I can first con-firm that I hear you have a need for rest (or whatever else I guess you need). Since I still want to have my needs (in this case of community and recreation) met, I continue to communicate about them, but at the same time taking your needs into consideration.

3. There is always more than one way to meet needs.

When I hear that your needs are an expression of freedom of choice, I propose a strategy that I believe can meet both your needs as well as my needs for companionship and recreation. We may choose any of these strategies:

- You work on your project and I will go swimming with someone else.

- I will help you with your project, or anything else that frees up time for you and then we can together go to swim.

Relationship evaluation - Part 5
Handling a "no"?

You can do this part of the evaluation, as a way to learn how to handle a situation when it is a challenge for you to either say no or hear a no. You can use it to find recurring challenges around "no".

Dealing with 'no' from others

15a. Is there anything you would like to ask for from the other person that you hesitate to ask for in fear of receiving a "no" from them?

b.   Which of your needs, do you hope to have met by what you ask for?

c.   What needs do you think are behind a possible 'no' from the other person? What needs do you guess this person is trying to meet by saying "no"?

d.   Do you see some other ways to get your needs met?

e.   Do you see some strategies that could meet all of the above needs being met? (Yours and the other person's).

Saying no

16a. Is there something you would like to say no to? Choose a specific situation that affects your most important relationships.

b. Which of your needs do you want to meet by saying no?

c. What needs do you think the other person wants to have your help in meeting, with his or her request?

d. Is there some other way to get your needs met than by saying no?

e. Are there some ways to get both yours and the other person's needs met?

Love as a feeling or Love as a need

"Do you love me?"
"When you say love, do you use it as a feeling or as a need?"
"As a feeling!"
"When?"
"Now?"
"No, I do not feel love right now, but ask me in a while and it may be different!"

The word love is a word used both to describe feelings but also to describe interpersonal needs. We sometimes use the dialogue above in our workshops in order to clarify the difference it can make for the connection between two people if they use the word love as a feeling or a need. It contributes to the clarity of communication if we are aware of and clear about how we use the word. When we use the word love to describe what we feel, it is often to describe that we feel hot, jittery, happy, excited or happy. Emotions change quickly. They give us information about what we are doing moment-by-moment. If the other person is using the word love as a feeling, be prepared to be disappointed because feelings change quickly. When we use the word love to describe something that all people need, it will have a different impact on our connection. Love is a need that we all share and when we talk about love, it's often a description of whether these needs are being met or not. It may include the needs for closeness, trust, belonging, acceptance, respect, emotional security and care. The word love is sometimes surrounded by "mystery". We talk about love as something mysterious

that cannot be explained and this can make it more difficult to get our need for love met. I want to suggest that love can be simple and very practical – nevertheless very sweet – and that we can take action on meeting this need in our daily life.

Ask yourself:
When did you last do something to meet your need for love?
What is your favorite way to meet your need for love?

Some tips to nurture relationships

- As often as possible ask, "What can I do to enrich your life?"

- Ask for appreciation when you need it.

- Express appreciation and gratitude you feel.

- Transform labels and diagnoses into observations, feelings, needs and requests.

- Transform demands into requests.

- Transform unspoken expectations to preferences.

- Take responsibility for your need for love being met.

- Ask for what you want, and if you get a no, ask for something else that can meet the same needs or ask for the same thing of someone else.

- Remind yourself that a no is a yes to something else. Take "no" as an invitation to further dialogue and a reminder that there is a chance to meet more needs by continuing to connect.

Mistakes - doors to deeper connection

When something goes wrong in an important relationship, it is useful to have a way to repair the connection. It could be when someone has made a "mistake" that led to reduced trust and goodwill. It could also be that a number of little recurring things have led to less warmth, love and companionship in the relationship. Instead of putting our focus on what could repair the trust, many of us do what we are most trained at, we look for whose fault it is, and we try to find a scapegoat.

I met an acquaintance, Erik, and saw at once that there was something going on with him. He confirmed it and told me that he had just broken up with his girlfriend Maria. She had had sex with another guy and when Erik heard this he immediately broke off the relationship. When I asked why he left her he said, "But she has been unfaithful, what do you think?"

I listened to him and the despair he expressed about how he felt a lot of warmth and love when he thought of her. But also I heard him say that what she had done was absolutely unacceptable.

It was painful to see, as it was clear that his action was intended as a punishment for her, but it was maybe him who was suffering the most. It was also clear that he - if he would ever be interested in "forgiving" or even "accepting" what had happened - would need to be heard in the depths of his own pain.

After speaking through more of his pain he said: "I do not understand how she could do this to me." I heard this as an opening to wanting to understand her and her motives. I also heard expressions such as "I thought I knew her, but obviously I did not" as evidence that he had no concept of what had driven her. Therefore he would probably find it difficult to shift his "enemy image" of her unless he could first understand the needs she had tried to meet through having sex with another person.

Trust is not built by trying to find out what is wrong. Trust is built through a combination of things: being heard, being received, but also by getting a response from others on how they are affected by our reactions to their choices and to understand why the others have done as they have. Genuine forgiveness can seem almost like magic, because it can heal wounds we had not dreamed were possible to heal.

A true 'sorry' is preceded by an experience of empathic contact and understanding.

I am suggesting a different way to say "sorry" than many of us are accustomed to. First, we listen to the other with empathy until she or he feels completely understood. Second, we try to really take in what the other is saying and express how it affects us to do so. Only after this, do we express how this is for us to hear. We can then mourn the choices we have made; now when we fully understand the implications of how what we did affected the other person.

Third, after we have heard them, the other person usually would like to hear why we acted the way we did, which of our needs we tried to meet in doing what we did. Only then will an "explanation" of what motivated us be okay for the other to listen to.

Many of us try to give explanations before we listen to the other. When someone is upset about something that hurt them, it rarely creates connection if we start by explaining ourselves. It is easy to hear this as an excuse or a defense and that we are not ready to face the consequences.

She or he may even experience it as another "violation", having to listen to you before you have heard how painful something you have done has been for them. An "apology" that does not contain the above three elements can, instead of leading to reconciliation, be seen as a way of trying to "smooth things over". If what we say will have the effect we want, we first need to show that we are willing to really listen to the other, and take in how our choices have affected him or her. It also needs to be clear that you are willing to do what is necessary to restore trust and contact. This whole process can take weeks or months to handle.

To ask for forgiveness in this way is usually a fruitful way to handle conflicts. Sometimes in a conflict there is so much pain on both sides that you may need a third party, a mediator for help in hearing each other.

Saying you are sorry

Step 1. Listen and try to really take in how what you have done has affected the other person. Focus on what the person is feeling and needing, rather than what he or she thinks about you or what you did. Remind yourself that you are not responsible for the needs of others being met, but you may want to contribute to it.

Step 2. When you take in what was said, express what you feel when you understand how your actions affected the other person. Focus on expressing the feelings that are stimulated by listening to him or her. Ask how it is for the other person to hear this. Possibly you will need to go back to step one again, especially if they hear your expressions as excuses.

Step 3. Express what needs you were trying to meet with what you did. It might be that there were needs that you were not aware of at the time. Make sure it does not sound like an "excuse" or that you are not responsible for your choices. Do not speak in a way that makes it sound like you are a "bad person" either as that may make the other person feel guilty. There is always a "good intention" behind your actions - as you were trying to meet your needs. Express what motivated you to act as you did, even if you have realized what the consequences were for the other person. Express it little by little and go back to the question of how it is for the other person to hear what you are saying. This may mean going back to both stage 1 and 2 when you are half way through. The processes to re-build trust might take time

Appreciation keeps relationships alive

Appreciation is a way to give and receive energy. It infuses joy into a relationship and is an opportunity to experience meaning and connection. Twenty years of research by independent researchers has shown that creating happy relationships is due to a particular balance between positive and negative communication. In relationships that people experience as happy, around five positive things for every negative thing is found. It is easy to forget to express appreciation to loved ones, to take them for granted. We think they understand that we appreciate them. But even if they do, most people still appreciate it when it is put into words. Interestingly, research shows that one of the things that distinguishes sustainable relationships is how we relate when the other person is happy. When we feel happy that things are going well for the person close to us and express this, it creates a sense of connection that helps us when life feels tough.

Besides the fact that appreciation spoken to our loved ones will strengthen our relationships, we also feel good when we express appreciation.

When you have just fallen in love with someone, it is easy to focus on what works and to express what you like about him or her.

When you have met a new friend, or when someone inspires you it might be easy to express appreciation.

But after a while, anywhere from a few days, weeks or months, we usually begin to discover more about the challenges in any given relationship. We begin to get a more nuanced picture of the other person. And for a while we may only see the negative. We might no longer see anything of what we appreciated so much in the beginning. We may even begin to see the very thing we appreciated in the beginning as negative. To balance our unmet needs it is supportive, every now and then, to focus on what we do appreciate.

It is a choice that gives a lot of energy especially if we put our attention on expressing certain things when we express gratitude.

First, the most important thing about appreciation is to express it. If you also want to increase the energy in your appreciation, follow the advice below:

1. Express observations of what you have seen or heard the other person do or say that you appreciate. Be as specific as possible so the person can recognize themselves in the situation you are referring to.

2. Express what you feel, when you see or hear what the other person says or does, that you appreciate. Express it as clearly as possible and let the other person receive the warmth in your feelings. Describe what this person has done that has affected you and talk about yourself instead of putting positive labels on him or her.

3. Express what needs these feeling are connected to. In what way does it take you one step closer to what you are longing for? What is nourished in you by what she or he has done?

Express how the other person's choices have nurtured your dreams or helped you to keep your hopes up. Express how the person's actions have enriched you and your life in a large or even in a small way.

Do Part 6, on next page on your own or with someone close to you.

Relationship evaluation - Part 6
Appreciation and gratitude

An appreciation that would make you "dance for joy"

Step 1

17a. Write down an appreciation you would really like to hear from a particular person. An appreciation you have not received (or did not receive as many times as you would have liked).

b. Imagine reading out loud what you have written for this person and then ask yourself;
"How is it that you have not expressed it before?" (Or not expressed it this way.)
Listen for the feelings and needs behind their answers. Perhaps this can give a clue as to why you have not heard this.

c. Write down an appreciation you believe a person close to you would be "dancing for joy" if he or she got to hear.
Select an appreciation you have not expressed before, or one you have expressed but that you are not sure that the other has been taken in.

d. Ask yourself:
"What would I need in order to express this appreciation directly to this person? Is there anything I can ask of her or him that would make it easier? "

Step 2

Share with the person concerned. Tell them you have explored appreciation and how you express or ask for it. If you want to , you can show what you have written .

Remember that for the other person this may be a new and strange experience. Therefore you may want to take it slowly and go step by step. Remember that the most important thing is your connection. Maybe you want to ask each other for more appreciation.

Step 3 - Reflection

Use some time for yourself to reflect on what you've learned, about yourself, about appreciation and gratitude, about relationships and about the other person.

Write down what you have learnt so that you can go back to it when you need inspiration.

Me, we and all the others

"Love relationships are beloved arenas for private bottlenecks and conflicts. Two lovers can never on their own correct what many generations before them have created."
Dieter Duhm[5]

In Sweden, a family with two parents and two to three children is seen as the norm. A "normal" teenager moves away from home because it's "healthy" to live by oneself for a while. Then, at any given time you should find a partner, preferably one of the opposite sex, in order to have children and start a family.
I have nothing against this way of living, but it worries me to see how

---

5 http://www.tamera.org/english/index.html

we relate to this norm as "the only way to live." It easily leads to judgments of those who choose to live in other ways. We forget that less than a hundred years ago many generations often lived in the same household. In many parts of the world people still live in "extended families".

No matter what we think about different ways of living, it is useful to realize that we do not have much experience with living in "single households" or even in small families. For many generations, yes, actually all the way back to the beginning of humankind, we have been living with people from previous generations or larger groups of people.

If we want to choose to live outside the norm, outside of monogamous and heterosexual relationships, there are often both internal and external pressures challenging the relationship. I have chosen to live "outside the box" in certain periods of my life and know how much energy can go into dealing with real or imagined reactions from others. But although they were challenging, these experiences also gave me a lot of very special gifts.

When we fall in love with a person we might not think about just how many people we are actually starting a relationship with. To begin with, there is the other person's parents, perhaps siblings, and then of course, close friends. It can spiral out to include the larger family of relatives, all which may impact on your relationships in small or large ways.

A relationship between two people always involves more people, which is perhaps more evident in cultures with so-called arranged marriages. Although it may not be so apparent in all relationships. Two (or more) families come together as well as the two individuals who have fallen in love. And with that joining comes a variety of assumptions and ideas about life, relationships and love.

As Duhm says in the quote above, love relationships become arenas in which we try to manage our "individual bottlenecks". In a close relationship very often our own challenges and things we have not been able to sort out show up. We might show more of ourselves but in a way that is challenging for others so we get stuck.

In a close relationship we often have demands (of ourselves and others) that we should "dare to be ourselves" and be open about ourselves. The other person should then - if she or he loves us - accept and deal with us just "the way we are."

This might sound good, But if we believe that the other person is there to always give us acceptance and to love us, the pressure on our partner often becomes too great. Discovering that it is a challenge for our partner to handle everything that goes on within us, we may leave the relationship in disappointment.

Our personal pain can also become the basis for reoccurring quarrels. And since we are focusing on the relationship and not on managing our own pain, the quarrels never end. I have heard many people say that they have discovered that although they have "exchanged the object of their love," the quarrels look the same. We always take our own selves with us into the next relationship. And as long as we do not get support to deal with self-criticism, shame or fear of being intimate, it will follow us into any relationships we enter into.

To be told "you're the only one who can understand me" can be very flattering at first, but to be "the only one" that can support someone can be stressful in the long run. To love someone is not the same as being able to manage all of their reactions to what we do or say.

No matter what kind of relationship we're talking about, it will be vulnerable if it is dependent on "the two of us" handling all of the pressures the relationship is exposed to. We need other people as well. There is a saying - "it takes a village to raise a child". I feel something similar goes for close relationships - "it takes a village to create a working relationship between two people." We need "Vitamin F" as in friends. Not only for support but also for inspiration from different sources. However, look out for "good friends" who are always on your side.

Be aware of the negative effects it can have to only have "good friends" who are always on your side. If you share your pain from a close relationship with someone that sympathizes only with you, you risk becoming blind for what you are responsible for. To receive sympathy can give you a distorted view on your relationship, so make sure that you get empathy and honesty when you receive support.

- He is so inhuman, I do not know how to stand it!

- Poor you, you deserve something better.

- Yes, but isn't it strange that he does this all the time.

- No, it's typical of men.

You would be better served by someone who helps you take in consideration both yours *and* the other persons needs. This person can encourage you to take more responsibility for what you are take responsible for. What I suggest is that you find a friend who can hear you and support you, instead of supporting the idea of the other person as inhuman, bad, or an enemy.

- He is so inhuman, I do not know how to stand it!

- It sounds like you are worried and have a need to experience care and warmth in your connection?

- Mostly I long for love. But don't you think it strange that he does this all the time?

- Is it that you are confused and want to understand? Would you like to ask him to give some information as to why he makes the choices he does?

- Yes, I do not know how to reach him anymore!

- It sounds like you really want to find a way to create connection? Would you like to hear some ideas I have about what might be going on within him?

What support do I have to take care of important relationships?

Do I have friends I can easily reach when I need them?

Do I nurture the connection with my friends? In what ways?

Do I listen when they say "truths" I'm blind to?

Relationship evaluation - Part 7
Meeting needs

Do the last part of the evaluation together with the person you are evaluating your relationship with. If you want, you can start with reflecting on the needs below, each by yourself for a few minutes. Begin with the needs you found most important in Part 1.

Remember that needs can be met in many ways and that they are not tied to a particular person, place, action or time. Allow yourself to think outside the "box" and make sure that any new strategies you might choose also meet other needs. Sometimes there are multi-strategies: strategies that can meet several needs simultaneously. (For example, to exercise together or eat dinner together will meet both the needs of community and of nurturance or movement.) Also focus on celebrating what actually works by expressing appreciation for the action that meets the needs. If you decide that you want to try new strategies to meet needs, make sure that you both feel the change is voluntary.

You can do part of the evaluation, with the whole family, with multiple partners if you are in so-called polygamous relationships, or with several friends.

Make sure everyone has space to talk and if you like, use the three following questions as support.

18. What do we do in our relationship to meet each of the following needs?

What could we do to meet them even better?

Are there any requests we want to express to ourselves, to each other or to someone else?

Intimacy

Respect

Safety

Freedom

Community

Honesty

Understanding

Inspiration

To have fun

Unity

To be seen and heard

Love

Meaning

Other needs

How internal images and external structures affects relationships

There is probably no theme more popular for books than that about love and relationships. There are an enormous amount of books with everything from pickup techniques, on how to decipher male and female language, books about sex, intimacy and communication.

I think one of the reasons why these kind of books attract such big interest is that most intimate relationships are founded on assumptions that make it difficult to create truly loving and respectful relationships. We have so many preconceived ideas about something that is so precious to us, and need support and inspiration to handle it. But if we never get to the core assumptions we have about relationships I am worried that books, (however inspiring) and communication tools will be of no use.

I have summarized some of the assumptions that I have often heard, expressed verbally or non verbally when I have supported people facing major challenges in their lives and relationships. These assumptions apply to all types of relationships. Relationships involving romantic and sexual expression seem to be the ones where we mainly get stuck in static ideas.

One assumption is that we only have sex with the person we are closest to, or with whom we have the most important relationship with. Imagine that something we previously called a "friendship" now also includes a sexual connection. Do we now start calling it something else, like - a romantic relationship? And are we then automatically changing the expectations we have of ourself and the other person? Can we be sure that the other person also is changing expectations and behavior just because *we* put another label on our connection?

The assumptions on the next page are not "truths". But I do hope they help you to challenge your learned ways of looking at relationships and to rethink them if you see that it can benefit you. Ask yourself if any of these assumptions have contributed to making your relationship a challenge and therefore valuable to reconsider.

Some usual assumptions about relationships:

- All relationships can be divided into categories (such as an acquaintance, a friend, a lover, or a partner).

- Each category has clear distinctions and roles to be followed.

- Every relationship can only belong to one category (at least within a certain time frame).

- To care about someone means that you care less about someone else.

- Love means that you have no control. Therefore, it is a dangerous condition.

- Every relationship is separate from all others.

- When something does not feel good in a relationship, it is handled by finding out whose fault it is. Then that person either will ask for forgiveness, or is excluded or punished in some other way.

Other possible ways of looking at relationships

- Every relationship is unique and different from the rest, no matter what we call it.

- Each person is free and at the same time, each person is mutually dependent upon others.

- Relationships change all the time.

- To care about or love a person can not damage the relationship with another person. It may even contribute to more needs being met in the relationship.

- Every relationship is intimately connected with all other relationships.

- When something does not feel good in a relationship, it is handled by attempting to re-connect, or by acting in the direction towards what you want to see more of in the relationship.

Relationship evaluation - Part 8
Clarity in intimate relationships

Hopefully, the earlier parts of the relationship evaluation made it obvious how important it is to be clear about what we feel and need, in order to know what we want to ask for in our most important relationships. This section contains various ideas for how you can continue to communicate on the basis of feelings and needs. You can use the lists of feelings and needs on page 26.

1. Preparing for important conversations

Use the following questions to prepare yourself for a conversation with someone about your relationship.

How:

Turn to the page with need words on page 27. Choose:

1. Three words for need that you experience are met in your relationship.

2. Three needs you would like to have met more in your relationship.

   Then do the same thing and guess what needs the other person would choose for both of these points.

Ask yourself:

- In what way do I want to share what I have chosen, to the other person?

- What would help us connect?

- What can I do so that the needs I have chosen are more likely to be met?

- What requests do I want to express to myself?

- What requests do I want to express to the other person?

- What requests do I want to express to someone else?

- Is there any appreciation I want to express? Are there some needs that are met that I want to share my gratitude around?

2. Communication with focus on connection

Communicate with a focus on creating a deeper connection (maybe around a challenging situation). You might prepare yourself with the questions above. Start by briefly describing the situation so that it is clear that you're talking about the same situation. For example: "When the children ask for a ride to their friends" or "When my mother comes to visit."

Take some time and let each person reflect on what needs are met or not met in this situation and how you feel. Make sure there is time enough for both to express this. Ask each other clarifying questions if you do not understand what this situation is like for the other. When you have a sense of connection and the needs are clear, find out if there are ways to meet everyone's needs.

Relationship training

Although I am pleased with the support that this book can provide, there are limits to what a book can do. Therefore, I'm offering training programs around relationships together with my partner, Kay Rung. This training attracts parents and adult children, partners, siblings, colleagues, friends, newly married couples as well as those who have been together for 40 years. Participants come on their own or together with another person. Some participants live in relationships, but attend the training on their own. We focus both on what works in relationships and on what one wants to change. The training includes:

- How we can express love, even when we have thoughts that he or she does not deserve it.

- How to be honest in charged situations.

- How we can create intimacy, even when it is a challenge.

- Finding the balance between freedom and mutuality.

- Creating intimacy that deepens the connection.

- How to identify and transform enemy images and static thinking.

- How to deal with anger, shame and guilt.

- Becoming aware of what we can ask for in order to experience more care, respect and love in our lives.

See our website www.friareliv.se/eng for trainings and how to organize a training with us.

References and literature

Eisler, Riane (1998), The Chalice and the Blade: Our History, Our Future. Harper.

Eisler, Riane (1996), Sacred Pleasure: Sex, Myth, and the Politics of the Body. Harper.

Isdal, Per (2001), Meningen med våld. Gothia publishers.

Larsson, Liv (2012), Anger, guilt and shame, three sides of the same coin.

Larsson, Liv (2009), Led som du lär. Ledarskap med Nonviolent Communication.

Larsson, Liv (2008), A Helping Hand. Mediation with Nonviolent Communication ISBN: 978-91-976672-7-2

Liedloff, Jean (1986), Continuum Concept. The search for the lost happiness. Da Capo Press.

Lerner, Michael (2000), Spirit Matters. Hampton Roads Publ. Company.

Lyubomirsky, Sonja (2008), The How of Happiness: A scientific guide to happiness. Penguin.

Powell, James (1974), The Secret of Staying in Love. Argus Communications.

Rosenberg, Marshall (2007), Nonviolent Communication, a Language for Life. Puddle Dancer Press

Rosenberg, Marshall (2008), We can work it out. Puddle Dancer Press

Rosenberg, Marshall (2005), Speak Peace In A World Of Conflict, What You Say Next Will Change Your World. Puddle Dancer Press.

About the author

Liv Larsson has studied relationships as a mediator and mentor for people in crisis. She also leads the course "Relationship Evaluation ". In addition, she has been exploring relationships within and outside the norm and has found that close relationships can be a source of personal growth and joy.

She is a certified trainer with CNVC (Center for Nonviolent Communication). She educates and mediates both in Sweden and internationally and teaches mediation and conflict resolution in various contexts.

Liv has written more then ten books on Communication, including, 'A Helping Hand. Mediation with Nonviolent Communication.

In the past few years she has specialized in Communication trainings based on "anger, shame and guilt."

She has translated Marshall Rosenberg's books into Swedish. Together with Kay Rung she regularly leads relationship evaluations for couples, friends and families.

Find out more about Liv on www.friareliv.se
About NVC and Center for Nonviolent Communication.
www.cnvc.org

Short tips to nurture your relationships

- Ask as often as possible, "What can I do to enrich your life?"

- Ask for appreciation when you need it.

- Express appreciation and gratitude you feel.

- Transform labels and diagnoses into observations, feelings, needs and requests.

- Transform demands into requests.

- Transform unspoken expectations to preferences.

- Take responsibility for your need for love being met.

- Ask for what you want, and if you get a no, ask for something else that can meet the same needs or ask for the same thing of someone else.

- Remind yourself that a no is a yes to something else. Take "no" as an invitation to further dialogue and a reminder that there is a chance to meet more needs by continuing to connect.

Try this advice for two weeks and put the list on your refrigerator.

www.ingramcontent.com/pod-product-compliance
Lightning Source LLC
La Vergne TN
LVHW011338080426
835513LV00006B/424